EX
VOTO

FRANCES MAYES

Frances Mayes

LOST ROADS PUBLISHERS
NUMBER 42   351 NAYATT ROAD, BARRINGTON, RHODE ISLAND 02806   1995

The author and publishers would like to acknowledge the following
publications in which some of these poems first appeared:

The Atlantic Monthly: "The Sacramento Street Wash-N-Dry"

The Chronicle of Higher Education: "The Sleeper"

College English: "Spring Equinox"

Colorado Quarterly: "Malaria/Palimpsest"

Domestic Crude: "Net"

The Gettysburg Review: "Etruscan Head" and "The Long Bony Cats of Montecatini"

Indiana Review: "Lullaby" (titled here "Ninnananna from Rignano")

Iowa Review: "Good Friday, Driving Home" and
"When Rain Pulls the Wind off the Arno at Night"

Ironwood: "In the Summer"

Manoa: "This Morning They Read 'Loveliest of Trees. . .'," "Devotion" and "Rubric"

The Mississippi Review: "To Begin the Migraine"

New American Writing: "Green Thoughts," and "Lines for Massimo"

North American Review: "Denouement"

North Dakota Quarterly: "In Benito Juárez Park"

Poetry: "The Untying of a Knot"

The Southern Review: "Ancient Air: A Stony Sestina, Doubled in Time,"
"Midsummer," and "Shaving My Legs with Ockham's Razor"

Volt: "Waiting for Grace (Believing in Waters)"

The Women's Review of Books: "Come Slowly Eden" and
"By the Mediterranean, Early Morning"

ZYZZYVA: "Lighting Candles to the Household Gods"

"The Book of Summer," section three, was published in a fine-press
limited edition by The Heyeck Press. The author thanks Robin Heyeck.

A National Endowment for the Arts fellowship was granted to the author
during the writing of these poems and she appreciates the support.

Library of Congress Cataloging in Publication Data
Preassigned card number 94-073273
Mayes, Frances
Ex Voto

Published by Lost Roads Publishers, 351 Nayatt Rd., Barrington, RI 02806-4336
Cover art: Sculpture studio, by unknown photographer, Costa Rica,
from the collection of Quinton Duval

*This project is supported in part by a grant from the National Endowment for the Arts
in Washington, D.C., a federal agency. Please advocate for public arts funding.*

For Ed

For adoration seasons change.

"A Song to David"
Christopher Smart

Table of Contents

I

Each of us gives or takes heaven in corporeal person,
for each of us has the skill of life.

Letters
Emily Dickinson

Midsummer

Now I see this field of potato vine and asphodel is not
as secret as I thought last night when we spread
the white blanket under the blanket of stars,
when we made love, made sex, made love,
made the ground furrow under us as though ready
for planting. We did not mean to fall asleep,
to stay outside all night, dew soaking us
with the grasses, the moon precisely halved.
I see the field is open, you asleep, and there,
so close, a farmer raising a sack as he looks this way,
stunned to see me pull on a shirt. The black dog
starts to bark so hard his forelegs leave the ground.
Wake up, my love, he is coming, though the sun
rises behind him, cutting him into a fan of light.

Spring Equinox

I'm eating the supper of a solitaire—
ice cream from the container with a fork.
From all the galaxies, a glint of light on the tines.
For no reason, the word *rood* forms in my mouth
as Jupiter rises above the chestnut tree's thousand
candles. Isn't this fine—merry silver moon, planet
spangling against the sky I lean into from my porch?
Now night starts to lose fast, as when the pharaoh was born
and workers began to cut stone for his tomb in the desert.

I want to know the source of *rood,* fresh to me from Jupiter.
Old gods may be convening, climbing meridians
as my blood runs a charted cycle, canals, lacunae,
all the underground river beds.
It's spring and death comes again to the pinned body
and we roll the stone, just when windflowers
in the weeds confirm innocence. Is this true?
A *rood*, placed to vex or unhex the season of joy?
And at year's end, dead end: miraculous birth

came to the woman closed out.
Among steaming flanks, thick smells of wool and dung,
she opened her legs and damp straw started to shine.
One sharp cry set the quick days on a swing
toward light. Oh, I'm just feeling the rising and falling
meter of stars. *Rood*, cross, and our sun is crossing
the celestial equator, bringing days I love.
I thought holy days had no meaning unless
the events were true. But to talk back

to nights without end did we make the gods?
If so we are wise. Out of the Pacific, salt fog comes
in waves black and wet. I'm tracking the plane
we are assigned or thrown to. I'm not penitent or pilgrim
but any old primitive looking at the universe.
If there's a God dotting lines along spheres for the sun
to cross, good. And if not, we are more
than we know. I can hold the windflower and
the crucifix nail in mind at once. I wanted truth

and find we form the words we need from flesh.

Rubric

The dining room is occupied territory:
Amaryllis! More striking than a person.
Eight red trumpets—
We expect La Marseilles to blare out
At midnight. These bright soldiers
Ten-gun salute us all day.
The petals curl out big as cow tongues,
Redder. I would like to call Nolde,
"Emil, over here right away,
Bring your sable brushes."
These blooms are my blood type, A-negative.
Green sword leaves look only
Compositional, tangential to the explosion.
The tough two stalks are thick as windpipes.
Each bloom unfurls and we pledge
Allegiance. Not even an artery opened
Squirts such red. Lustrous velvet Valentine,
A dizzy swirl, all nouns used as verbs.
Eight from one bulb. North, South,

East, West, the cardinal points times two.
Can this beauty be accidental?
The red carousel may begin to spin us.
The veins turn indigo. A sheen of iridescence,
As on oily rain and a parrot's head,
Casts on my hand as I come near.
How can this die? How can this go on?
Everyone comes to drink a few carmine
Gulps. I want to start
Conversations, "Your turn to cut the cards,"
Or, "Let me take you to lunch."
Who sang "Sweet Amaryllis, winsome
Country maid"? This redoubtable, amaranthine
Red queen is a jazz singer riding a riff.
She sings the low notes, my Belladonna Lily.
Here's Beauty, acting as its own state's witness,
Redeemed, a thunderclap of red.

The Sleeper

The man in the flat below starts to snore,
broad vibrations travel through
the floor, box springs, into my pillow,
sine waves that could snap the Golden Gate.
He's sawing off sequoias, a steady buzz,
sharpening as it cuts rings of years and hits the heart.
What if I had to lie beside a platypus like that?
Soft palate flapping like a red towel in the wind.
I try to scan the noise, it's certain I won't sleep:
shonk, shee, shonk, shee, caesura, shonk, shee, shonk, shee,
trochaic tetrameter snort,
his lines broken by fut-fut spondees.
Is his wife turned, lonely, on her side, wondering
how lush desire changed into this deep ache
to push peanuts up his nose?
This seems more like *grand mal* seizure than sleep.
When the REM slows, his rhythm shifts: two geese
honk and squawk—barnyard traffic jam.
She lies beside him in earmuffs watching
lamps shake in the moonlight each time bullbreath charges.
Poor moon goddess to this Endymion of glottal stops.
Will she drift to the sofa, trailing
an afghan some aunt made for other atavistic nights?
Wide awake, I drop *The American Heritage Dictionary*
from six feet and the rusty motor of the turboprop stalls,
adjusts its flight pattern. A light whir now,
cropduster grazing tall treetops.
Awake, could he perform these feats?
Turn in his junk bond job and become
some nasal cyberpunk synthesizing his bleats?
Right now he's composing a classic
"Sonata for Tuba Filled with Water."
My bed in the dark lists as though dragging anchor.
Close under the bow, a sperm whale wheezing
and snorking through his dorsal blowhole.
I wrap my arm around my ears, brood
on the thin membrane of civilization.
Below, Neanderthal man in skins, sated on bear blood,
rests from the hunt in a four poster bed.

To Begin the Migraine

Rain starts to prickle my scalp.
I lie back as if boneless.
The equator tightens its wire.
I want the fog heaving above the roofs
to be still, the clock to calm down.
Balloons press tight skins against the ceiling.
Please, take away your vivid face. Go,

make cockaleekie soup—don't
ask me the etymology of "migraine."
I'm letting the bloodroot grow
its single pale flower.
The blanket scratches, irritates,
the dog breathing and breathing,
everything insists, even sky,
lavender through the white swell
of curtain. A sweet domestic air
tries to fill the corners. Ache,

ache, I say, soft enough to be calling
a gray animal from under a bush.
My own feet are so far away.
Go, wash the grains from leeks,
watch the pearl barley roil.
Tracks are joining, the gold spike
driven in. I have two wild cowlicks,
I'm the left-handed child, skull
hot with fault lines. You're outlined
in neon, your voice breaking over me.
I'm within this. I won't be
stopped from riding bareback
under the immense tent of gauze.

Sister Cat

Cat stands at the fridge,
Cries loudly for milk.
But I've filled her bowl.
Wild cat, I say, Sister,
Look, you *have* milk.
I clink my fingernail
Against the rim. *Milk.*
With *down* and *liver*,
A word I know she hears.
Her sad miaow. She runs
To me. She dips
In her whiskers but
Doesn't drink. As sometimes
I want the light on
When it is on. Or when
I saw the woman walking
Toward my house and
I thought *there's Frances.*
Then looked in the car mirror
To be sure. She stalks
The room. She wants. Milk
Beyond milk. World beyond
This one, she cries.

Pond (oral)

      Mouth opens
so   whole

                  bound   aureole

      (*lake* shallow quick and naked
sea the stretched to infinity. . . .)

dropped
               pond

with green slider turtles
—fate's in the dime store—

(creeks are tinny, streams sublime)

      oxygen forming
      crack of alligator jaws, sluice of water through serrated teeth
      pods of seed let loose to carry

p small pucker   no wonder no moss

even an echo of the frog

     at night   *o, n, d,*

deep breath bottomless nonetheless
               aluminum pie plate glints there

Vigil

Sometimes his chest hums like the freezer where my mother kept her shelled peas in white cartons and my father kept the body of a deer.

Sometimes a night bird with reptilian head pecks at the windowpane then, frantic, flutters and pecks reflections all over the glass.

I must sleep sometimes.

Sometimes his little snore sounds like someone trudging up the stone stairs.

What keeps me awake at home: the sudden rip of a car alarm set off by a cat jumping on the warm hood of a black Saab, or set off by a three-point earthquake or by project boys prying the door for the tape player. Or the recycle truck's cascade of shattering, green fragments of wine bottles arching into the open chute, breaking glass behind my eyes. Or the child downstairs, crying to be taken into her parents' bed, to fall into that warm slot between two bodies. Tumor on the brain stem. Trajectory of the bullet through my father's body. Mother as a flapper hanging over my head, the nail weak in the plaster. The violation that occurred to the most innocent one. The hand I would cut off if he still lived. The wattage of the moon. Harelip, broken neck, daylight and dishes life. The fabulous crown roast ringed with cranberries when I was in love with two men at the table.

you'll live to regret it

Or, I don't sleep because sleep doesn't exist. Hypnos is off banqueting late with brother Death and son, Night. Who is the wife, mother, goddess? Perhaps her real name is more beautiful than the word Insomnia but that is the only name we know. Her blue eyes always focus on the middle distance. She wears bracelets of stars and stands on a waning gibbous moon, her large feet firmly curved over the old moon's hunched back.

Sometimes the house will slide down the mountain and in the morning will be returned firmly to its bedrock, broom, and spruce.

He casts a seine of dreams but I swim out. He covers me with the swansdown quilt but I kick it off. He says, *It's the chalybeate time; your mouth tastes like the frozen faucet when I was a boy.* Then he falls, a feather down the chimney.

What keeps me awake here, 7,000 miles away—the idea of home, the travelling clot, the plunge of so many into the earth? My house—where strangers brew herb teas, who may be leaning against my pillows discussing acupuncture and car repairs. How can they take up their lives among my forks, books and mirrors. The place should disappear when I do; reappear when I return. What keeps me awake here—the lunar moth waiting for me to sleep so it can light on my leg. The Tuscan landscape pressing against the window. Skinny flared silhouettes of two palm trees. Tall procession of cypresses, each one planted for a dead soldier, winding along the white road. The dip of the valley that pulls the heart with it. Why miss a minute of the wobbly moon hoisting over St. Egidio? *My infant eyes . . . .* What keeps me awake —the name of the insect spray I can't think of. The name of the Welty novel that starts off with all those similes. One word begins with B. Chromosomes that need parental guidance, brain pan where the oil caught fire, those handfuls of placebos, fall through crazed ice, I pushed him I didn't push him down the stairs. He was slashed and held his intestines in with his own hands while they took down his name and work address. Speed reading at the deathbed, ambulance's mad race in the downpour, you crushing my ring into my fingers, code blue in the hall, gobs of blood dumping out the sump pump, I'm shouting my way out of sleep.

(Now there are guests and I feel their doughy breathing rising through the stairwell.)

What keeps me, what keeps.

Sometimes I rest my face against his back, imagining I have my ear on the Serengeti Plain; I hear herds of gazelles leaping, hooves piercing soft earth, they are almost to the flat lake.

Hypnos lies without moving in the mirrored chamber. He stretches across the voluptuous bed. Her side is propped with pillows. Beside the bed she has a table with a small clay tablet and a row of vials and glass pots, her unguents for luring sleep, potions for removing, smoothing. They are empty, wing of a dragonfly in the stone blue one. She tries to match her breath to his. In. In. Can't catch me.

Prescriptions for sleep: run through the happiest events of your life. List the most beautiful places you ever have been, putting yourself back in each one, experiencing, smelling, feeling the landscape that has stayed with you. Walk through the first house, every room. Prepare a meal (you liked her pot pie), take a bath, sit in the sling-back chair in the garden. What are you reading there under the lemon trees?

How hard he has to work at sleep. Coffee at midnight, he says, gives him strength to sleep. I sip tepid water. I have read every book in the world. How his breath rises, rises more. He twists his head and a slip of drool gathers in the corner of his mouth. He is breathing through his mouth hard now.

I expect his legs to quiver, like a dog running full out across a field in a dream.

Sometimes I am drifting and my body jerks, the way someone in an electric chair takes the first jolt. My nerves singe.

He flings his arm over me and suddenly he smiles. His look intensifies. He appears to be concentrating passionately on sleep. He must, he must, and it isn't easy. I stare, stare. I am frightened when his eyes rove. He looks comatose, maniacal. No, innocent. He looks so sweet, just as he used to when he was a boy and fell asleep on mama's afghan. If he were dead, we would say he looks as though he's sleeping.

Sometimes the telephone rings once: an electric eel slides through my brain.

Try the litany of the animals you've loved. Pet them again. Go up the steps where the albino deer is sleeping under the swing. Rub the knobs and coarse white hair. Slowly, leg joint by leg joint unfolds and the deer stands beside you, gently butting his head against your thigh. You stay with the deer a long time then you walk down the steps toward the marsh and the deer follows. It is good to walk toward the waving grasses with the deer beside you. The tide's saline rush rises in your mouth. Then the luxurious cat again curls along your outstretched arm, her purr buzzing into your wrist, her head resting in the cup of your hand. Your fingers sense her skull, nudge her ears, barely feel her small cat breath and the moist black pad of her nose. Let her sleep, her black fur length extravagantly extended along the pillow. And then the dog, the old one, into whose ear you whispered, *only you understand me*, the dog named Tish . . . .

Insomnia's emblem, a cup of warm milk she is pouring out into the sky where it forms a white veil behind our favorite stars. Insomnia and Hypnos make love every night. Immediately he falls into a godsleep and she scrubs all the clean floors and straightens the armoire where she keeps the clothes she never wears. Insomnia is naked, though at dawn she sometimes slips into a thin cotton shift embroidered with almond blossoms, flowering pear, jasmine stars, blooms she has steeped for her bath water. Hypnos blends easily into sleep. His skin is the color of obsidian, impenetrable as night, blacker than waters of sleep.

Sometimes I am rolling in sand.

Sometimes all the holy water fonts are dry. In the dusty scallops of marble, not a drop for my hot forehead.

"Three light over yellow and follow," he says. "What's yellow?" I ask. Incomprehensible answer, from his Sumerian life perhaps. Then clearly,

Campanile. In the well." A campanile has a bell in it and bell rhymes with
well and with the first syllable of yellow; follow almost rhymes. Is he hitting
a dip between his language center and his dream, a trough between waves?
This is the mystery of sleep, so easily forgotten.

I don't need to fall asleep. I'm not *here* when I sleep. I'm *there*.

I think of Kathy Fiscus who fell in the well when I was a child and we fol-
lowed it twenty-four hours on TV before she did not get saved. Run across a
corn field in Texas and disappear, falling down mossy sides, splashing of
dank water where snakes coil around your legs and frogs land on your
shoulders. Some wells are bottomless—hit the aquifer that joins all the
underground rivers of the world. Who will save you, not the shout at the
top of the shaft of light, not the slippery rope, not the everlasting sun cen-
tered for a moment far over your head.

Sometimes I am in the water under the Golden Gate bridge at night, just on
the surface, flailing, trying to clamber onto a rubber dingy while the neap
tide sucks the harbor out to sea. Fathoms and fathoms of pitchy water
under my scissoring legs. Is the sloop Primavera sunk, just at the gate?
F. already is on, reaching for me. I look way up and see the bridge over us,
the whir of cars and fast cutting blades of lights. His white flesh. Silence.
Swells lift us, then we fall fast. My body inseparable from the weight of
water, as though porous. I am rolling over the flimsy raft, just about on
when I wake up. I open the shutters. Gentle earth and air. The twelve lights
(one green) scattered around the crooked arm of the valley. Still weighted by
the pull of water, the force of it straining in me like a plane taking off. I feel
my hair and it is not wet.

He has curved around my back, his breath against my neck, his ambrosian
body shaped to mine, the skeletons at Pompeii, lovers surprised by lava gas
in their sleep.

Does he sleep because he's happy? Because the unwavering eye of god is
on him?

Sometimes sleep feels like early death and I get up with everything erased
from me except my airy barely existent body that hurts if I touch my skin,
my feet far away on the smooth floor.

Sometimes my heart's not in it.

Sometimes I'm a starfish poked with a stick.

In the Summer

In the long trip back,
In the hard visit,
In humidity,
In failure and impatience, and
Worn out with the living,
I drive my mother to the cemetery
To visit the still family.
I turn right at the Bryant plot
And on down the line
To find our name chipped in granite.
Are you cool down there
In your bones, old ones?
Ah, they're neglected:
Weeds, vases overturned.
My mother, who would not
Say so, is sweating.
My mother, who is
A large old baby,
Who has no memory to speak to.

The car ticks in the heat.
Last night I wrapped
A damp sheet around me
As if to break high fever.
I rinse the vase and
Fill it with water.
From here, I see her lurch
From the car, one hand
Clutching at air.
Bad doll to dress and feed,
Ancient bride, see, they've gone
Downstairs before you.
The glare from the slabs
Hurts her. The earth could open,
Poor husk, my tooth and claw.
The water smells like iron.
I will never forget anyone.
I see my mother
As she is now,
Squeezing hard the stems
Of the white, imperial chrysanthemums.

Malaria / Palimpsest

Living on tepid water in small sips.
Ribs sore, as though they could break through,
foreign, like the eighth-month child's elbow
shifting. The nuns wash my hair in a cold basin
while the war wounded in gray flannel walk the halls.
I am sick and my mind
has followed my body's achy lassitude.
I won't turn my head or form a word or a fist.
The mining goes on, the cauldron hot, axes swinging hard
into veins of ore, a fluttery yellow canary. Sister Anna
wants me to take a slow stroll along the parterre
and I don't answer but last night the ripped
scream came from my throat. He was on the stairs
again, bent, black stick figure who
reshapes himself for every nightmare.
Tell them my neck hurts against the cold basin.
I ran from the doctor, threw down the sharp covers
and took off down the hall, cornered by the big mawed
nurse grinning, soft as dough.

> Living, ribs could break through, sallow light,
> In small sips, foreign, bones sore, in a cold basin,
> Like the eighth month, of water tepid, the wounded
> Peer and nod, small shifting sticks, gray pajamas
> Walking the hall, I am sick and they wash,
> The mining goes on, she, the glasses of, she wants,
> Cauldron hot, wash my hair, I don't form, the limp
> Ache, the words, they wash, and my mind has followed,
> Cold axes swinging hard, a fluttery yellow canary,
> She wants a slow stroll, the word I want I ran from,
> The doctor, and wash my hair, the basin hurts,
> Swinging into veins, cornered in the hall, they lift me,
> My blood peppered with lead, the scream came,
> Against the basin, why won't my word, the black stick figure,
> Threw off the sheet, he reshapes himself, I don't
> Answer, sunken and icy, cornered, wild, the word won't,
> About to come for me, again, the cold basin,
> In every nightmare of my life, hands tarnishing the sheet,
> I can't make a fist, the wrong lens lengthening,
> My hair hurting, cornered, her mouth aluminum gaping teeth.

In Benito Juarez's Park

Will Benito Juarez in a black suit and starched collar stroll by with
Maximilian on his mind? Plumes of sunlight sway through leaves. Time
gone could come back. My sandal sinks in loam. Your father as an exchange
student buys the papaya on a stick, carved to look like a flower. Hear him
practice his hundred words of Spanish? Flounced skirts could sweep the
path. Egrets in the trees flap primordial wings, soar off for food for their
ugly young. Thud of basketball in the distance, blood throbbing in my
head, beating and chanting out of sight.

We could be farther back, the air green and musical. An old drunk pees
against the mimosa. The amaryllis throws out a faint vanilla scent. My feet
make lasting prints in mud. An old woman watches me in Spanish, her
hands swollen from her hundred years of work never done. Her lids hood
like a lizard's. I think we have something to do with each other but it is at
the layer of the bed of ashes. Upright we walk out of different worlds.
A stream of satiny water curving over moss.

Benito Juarez was just and drove around to think in his black carriage. He
felt the pity: Mexico, so far from God, so close to the United States. Calla
lilies glow from inside, immaculate as chalices. I come here late to think but
the park suspends me. How cool, the timeless. I'm swimming this green
aquarium too. The park gate shuts out all cause. The fountain plays four
notes of falling water. The horizon thrum of the woman's voice calling, full
fluttering of wings. The mud could slide off under my feet into another
layer. All darkens, a heliopause. Moss air, water trees, flute fountains,
ancient clay bodies in shadows. Light runs along the ground skimming the
tilted white rims of the lilies. Blue dragonfly on a coil of fiddlehead loosen-
ing into the sun.

Green Thoughts

1. Twenty-seven shades, most plump
                              plums and whorls
an incessant order of seed, pod, radiant
              flare opening like blowing glass
    but spiky   limp down the shadow into
                                   water. Cold

   cold
   circle
slab and check. Height to face
of sunlight and hands
                   endowed with brilliance,
brilliance, the sound shines!

                         The clay
circumference at a remove—but keeping
the borders "forever."
My politics: believing anyway
                             the shape
    of "to pour" in all languages,
                         an open invitation.

    Black belt dirt and verdigris: gradations
                         a silver flute accomplishes moving up
    air. Would you choose?

                         The words
                 square
boxes and smooth
                 lapis tiles. Rose swan
head drooped to exude
a warm spice.   Like writing lines, these
        touched with confidence: when tiles are blue
they feel
         like water clouds
                   pass through.

                   Take shadow angles on a gray
   drifting

       with the gloxinia forward
           as it should be. A flower

not to pick, as in literary. Labeled
gloxinia it is not now wild fox-

                              glove

  (with a petit sexual metaphor)
I mean

    not   hothouse not sweetsop not
    the key to a cipher
                      but a way.
Sycamine, cymling, the forked spines with edible scarlet berries.
Dirt and a flax seed.
           Clinch of rain.
And where it never stops.

2. See,
              the pleated shade spread.
              Everything
                      just as you never left it. See.

Almost that innocently we
        perpetuate

not lies. Safe qualifiers.

She speaks her mind, he said and I hoped
it was a compliment. Speak her mind.

Like eating toast with cinnamon sugar in the garden,
and shots fired beyond the fence.
                  If you can, believe.
If you can believe that, why
             it's a skip and a jump
             to the tiny mouse in the wainscoting,
             propped in matchbox bed,
             eeny paws clutch a yellow book.
    All in scale.

                 Mouse of the mind, what
are you reading?
        Pepy's plague year?

3. Woman in black bending over the page,

pages turning like waves, turning.

                    A pot of ink,
calligraphic scratch, one character
                meaning joy of life.
The voices pass, upholding the scene. Her curvilinear
coat,
        when I stare long
                a face
                                shifts, she's

unrecognizable to me, someone
                                else who was all along and
where does this leave us?

But I'd know your hand in a bucket of hands.

Trans
    substantiation. But she shifts.
I see her again as herself.
                            As *I* see her
(as a daughter quickly scans the letter of the accidental, the panic, the
dread, it's just *Mother*).   Still,

I imagine her.
            The unediting of her face
unfurling. Set down, the carafe ripples
                                wine years gone,
As in an aquarelle.
Her arms two Ls.
Her darkened borders.

4. Coda: un/theo/rhetorical.
Because the truth: we *know* why.
Directions: Go. Take something to plant in the new land.
Sidelight: Take and eat.
Memory: Shell, peel, fry. Flip. Turn that down.

It seems: Without the leisure of *it seems*.
Outlook: Diurnal.
Regret: Yes. Yet.
Greatest fear: Nobodaddy.
Credo: A breeze at the curtained door 3,000 miles south,
    a crude cage of birds, songs unforced and dusty, something

                            ancient
like the skill of life. Why? Concepts—

filial piety, pure arcs of thought,
                              black waterlilies
roots dense and twined

                    by the give and take
of the moon   I could step out on water,
        any minute contrary   walk, holding forth

II

I had my mother's picture in my shirt pocket and
I could feel it warming my heart, as if she were sweating too.

Pedro Paramo
Juan Rulfo

Real mysteries cannot be solved
but they can be turned into better mysteries.

Lipstick Traces
Griel Marcus

This Morning They Read "Loveliest of Trees...."

The dead can play the symphony tonight.
There's Frankie on second violin, pout
on her mouth, hair white as I might
expect, and my father years dead,
who'd know he played cello.
Rachmaninoff, logs rolling
in a river, tumult of sex in a feather
bed, the one classical I wore out in high school,

music that swells and spews, mudslide and fire.
All skeletons on their flutes
flash back to black and white
in soft harsh light. Frankie is the same name
as my mother, who lives yet. The dead Frankie
rides the big surf of romance tonight
unlike her funeral this morning
with the Carmelites plainchanting her
to their heaven, unlike
the priest with his wafer aloft.

Tonight all the refluent dead can play
tuba and tympani: Janice
with the gravelly voice, yes, Abby once more,
pull up what has rooted, so many,
my uncle who collected wildflowers, pulled down
last summer. The conductor waves his arms.

If he turned would he have a face?
Let them
connect with rapture again and
Mister Father, I don't want to go
down in the ground.
My body wants the buzz of light.
I want to be at Symphony Hall thinking
of a record club coupon
I forgot to mail years ago and
hence this particular music
plays me like a similar memory:
standing in the resurrection ferns at Angel Falls,
the cold cascades, all the fresh memories
run simultaneously, a current. A flash,

like applause. I balk at the whole notion,
God's friendly knee, Frankie telling him
a thing or two when she arose, that whoosh
of soul into the sky. There is nothing in it

for me or any Frankie whose wrist flicks not
her bow in the deep burst of the adagio.
I had to sit on the pew,
watch the symbolic candle and follow
Father's surety into overeasy consolation but
at the end the poem she chose said
look at the cherry tree hung with snow.
The music see-saws, pinpricks, agrees.
This morning I had to leave in

blaring red dress, crying, passing
people who stared and a white cat,
not a spirit at all,
who rubbed my leg as though sorry. Animal.

The Spanish say church in the morning, bullfight
in the afternoon and whorehouse at dark.
The music starts slow shifting, a large truck
going downhill in the Rockies. Frankie had

the touch of life. I hear her hit
the one false note of the night.

Good Friday, Driving Home

Not travelling; getting there. Traffic
Pouring into blinding light. But the fog
Looks enlightened, roiling over the hills—
Messengers might appear in a chariot
With news of the open-ended universe.
The groove I've worn down this road.
Back-lit sky, are houses near the coast
Blazing? My mind drags the pavement
Like a string of tin cans. There, horses,
Six, seven, grazing along the reservoir.
One is a palomino. Of course, of course
They remind me. The sight, ice on the heart.
Those lost could do worse than be recalled
By horses in spring grass, worse
Than own all shaded streets, lilacs,
And sailboats. Who do I think they are,
Saints, with their emblems? I'm affected by
This silvered sky, drastic day mad with
Traffic. Years gone I memorized Donne:

Restore thine Image, so much, by thy grace,
That thou may'st know mee, and I'll turne my face.
Westward, westward, things in motion stay in motion.
I roll down the window, watch for cars swerving
To the wrong lane. So many of us alone. Compact.
Good mileage. We fail and can tell ourselves nothing.
We break apart and invent
Why. We place our faith. Lose track. Blinker flashing,
Keep left. I am totally emptied and must
Fill myself again. The racing of powerful,
Unlovely emotions. What is the endless world?
Comes around again the cusp of summer.
I still like linen. Peach colored linen. I think
Of tanning my legs. I feel the word *prayer*
In my mind. Just the word. A smooth river stone.
I'm accomplishing the miles to San Francisco
For the thousandth time, add them to my vita.
I'm better off than Mona's mother with her hair
In curl papers thirty years, waiting for the occasion.
I have occasion. Press on. Oh soul of mud.
Half of what sacrifice ransoms us?

I Thought about You

Moon unusually brazen
In the left window. I watch it
Angle down and dim, then center
And I wish it would stop
For the night. Sleep's gone, sifted
Through me into the blue sheets. I think
I dreamed that dream again. If only a guardian
Angel would appear in the doorway, palm
Lifted, bringing the scent of heaven—
Gardenia and starched lace. What
Could she say but *aldilà*? You come back
Too often. Now that I've subtracted
Your name from mine, who can you be?
Not a friend, no one. Only the mind
Can *boggle*, the word reserved,
As in the way one says *my husband*.
A Creole conjure woman lived in this room.
I catch her faint zest of oranges.
Those are her calla lilies in the yard,

Clean white cones I could drink milk from.
Hard heels fast like yours
Clipping the concrete at this hour,
Some pale soul off early to work. Still it's night.
Sleep, night, night, sleep. There's a truth
If only I could uncover it.
A rude hex, a final word cut
In a gold medallion. If only
My room would fill with butterflies
And the thumb-sized finches
That nest in the eugenia bushes. Three, four,
Five. I might as well lower the bucket into
The well, myself into myself again.

Denouement

Naked, cool sheets, my hair
still damp, I will my face
to a center swirl, the glory
rose like Dante's idea of heaven.
My shoulders opening petals

edged with gold. Tips of my feet
stiffening into green stem.
I learned as a girl to be a rose
instead. For the force of bloom,
the steady iridescence.

The wrong moon.
That waxing gibbous diffuses
through the shade. Humpback
moon. I wish I thought in Latin.
The ablative, expressing removal,
direction from. I hear the white
china clink of his cup.
He's reading *Arctic Dreams*—
a white bear rises
but against white flurries. Only
the tongue and claws stand out.
Maw opens, fills with snow.
But his study is calm.
In thousands of books, black
words tick border to border.

Bright scenes inside the heart.
Shake the ball, the season changes
to winter. He is who he is.
Words, all from dead languages,
as in the stretched afternoons of childhood,
reading, hornets in the eaves,
grinding against the glass, buzzing
pages, the preterit, conjugation, knocking
into transparent skin, and all
I remember is *Do not spur a willing horse.*
Who says this? Someone marble.

I expect the print of his face
on my handkerchiefs. How far
can the night go.
I slip on the moon, a soft fall,
then I hear the page turn.
This night is a mirror
a cat looks into, seeing no one.

Net

I do not like you
walking through
the dark house
when I am sleeping.

You stand in the black
kitchen filling a glass
with tap water.
I am dreaming upstairs.

The skylight is like
a light at the top of a tomb
where someone lies
undisturbed for a thousand years.

The gauze netting falls
around my bed, another
level of sleep.
But you are slowly
drinking cold water.

Between us the quiet
is the black inside
closed books, the light
inside stems of flowers.
I want the sleep to last.

You put the key on the table.
Go, sleep
in your own empty house.
But where?

You walk through
like the movement
of a star from
the bottom of the world.

Inscriptions on a Ribbon in the Sky

In a stone sink on the roof, I wash my clothes.
Who am I? I could be pressed in another stratum.

Could look out on the white Crusaders as easily as I see
hombres with ragged flags walking toward the Virgin here.

The *hombres* know something I don't know. I don't know how to cut
a swath of my hair and pin it to the image that can save me.

I read everything about Palenque.
When I got there, nothing but silence to talk to.

I bought the 30,000,000-year-old fossil, big snail, black
logarithmic spiral turned to stone. What happens

in the long changes of the mind, that geology.
I only know I can stand in the aisle of the third-class bus

with Mexican torch music blaring, wind in my face,
weaving down the road and I don't care where

I'm going. The Woman in the Shawl of Dark Stripes presses
against my arm. Her hair hangs straight as wet wash.

Perhaps I always will remember her. Pebbles or topaz
may recall her steady eyes.

All I know is what I don't want to know.
Where is the next large space?

Someone thought he'd got there when he hung Padre Hidalgo's
head in a basket. But after ten years of swinging,

Hidalgo was hero again.
The long count was Maya time.

The waiter in El Trigal says, Just wait a Mexican minute.
A mask hid the mummy face at the bottom of the pyramid

at Palenque. Crackle jade with shell eyes, pupils
of obsidian. The black point eyes still stare though the real

are gone a thousand years. And Hidalgo's kitchen.
Bowls on the counter today. I could make tortillas.

A lemon tree in the courtyard blooms full of bees.
Of the great sights I've seen, one is the massive

many ton Olmec head with a tunnel carved through
the ear and out the mouth. Someone whispered

and those listening, the guide book insists, thought the stone
spoke. If Olmecs carved stone with no tool known,

they surely saw the little guy crouched on the left
holding forth. Maybe they chose to believe. Anyway.

I remember those choices. A belief in "forever."
The child I raised is writing in Spanish.

The man I married is looking out at the gray Atlantic
5,000 miles north of here and he is thinking of no one.

The one I was raised by props in a doorway watching
passersby. She thinks I am my sister.

The friend I walk with has a ticket in his hand, already
he's travelling around lakes in his mind.

There's a German word for the unrest of birds before
migration but I no longer know it.

I think of them all, hardening in time.
And the lacy trees I see from the roof are greatly

swaying, a unison, the human quality of gaiety flowing
against blank sky. On the opposite roof, a woman hangs wash.

Centuries may pass. The lifting of the white sheet and
the pinning it down. Spotted pigs in shade root and twitch.

The green view of hills is pulled by
my eyes, quick as filmstrip pulled across a light.

Landscape with no time in it and where are we?
I never understood my father when he said, Root, hog or die.

Four black turkeys strut the yard, fierce and oversized,
as in a child's Thanksgiving drawing.

The Untying of a Knot

Divorce, how ugly.
Ugly all the people.
Brutal their faces
and stunned, crude.
How stupid the broken family
like so many dropped
crates of gaily painted china
bought on holiday when you
imagined the meals at home,
at home, the wildflower
plates in the kitchen sun,
saucers for peaches and
ginger cream, rainy afternoon
with Chopin shaking the ficus,
the record with the deep scratch
but you don't care, and
the line of lemon trees
up the drive, yellow, yellow,
the right faces, mirror-to-mirror.

One nail drives out another.
How far to reality from here?
Names as close as your own
veer into other trajectories.
You enter a din, you're late,
main course already served.
And where were you
on the day everyone remembers?
How sentimental the future is,
all unearned. But the future,
you say, will have in it
me, me, me.
Wasn't it sad when that great ship
went down, hit the bottom?
You are the first family
to fall. This is a small sloop
and a long reach.
Quick-witted, you fit yourself
to the wind. You say
the Gulf is silky, aquamarine.

You are seen, suddenly
by the sun. You,
with similar fingerprints,
you, who walked up the rue du Paradis.
You're the short division of all,
owner of four forks, four chairs.

Aide-Mémoire: The Seventies

1. If I've had. The anger of youth. To take off. I was a woman. We had come to the group. We have suddenly. The initial feminist. It's disgusting. According to most. Wasn't our war. When I feel powerless. Eventlessness. Mother right. If hostility. I'm sick and tired . . . .   A process of the female. A terrifying. What's loose rolls west. I don't think you'll be very happy. A woman's liberty. Our legs, busts. The way we weave. Even the most freedom. Between your legs. Normal reaction. The *Times* congratulates Miss A, a petite brunette. Just imagine they are wearing. I had my children first. A mellowship in California. The man so big he can't ask for anything unless he's horizontal. Sort of laughed. It's not enough to do better. Who seem to shrivel. The trauma of. This is not a bedroom. It won't last six months.

2. No man would have welcomed. His tragedy and mine. No dancing. I'm not going to get. You can tell that bastard. Until the will of the. Frag that lieutenant. We've lost more over there. It isn't peace. It's almost. When anyone can say. This is a false ending. What's disturbing. We walked out. Suckers, having to risk. One time in Vietnam . . . . Vets are only. They didn't hear. The average crisis of energy. I would certainly prefer. Malcontents. Radicals. Incendiaries. The authority. A spoon of Mekong mud. A new feeling. It's not over. No, it's not over buddy boy. Turn out the lights and fuck, he shouted out over the lake.

3. At some point the United States. We have absolutely. Black budget, red ink. Under the doctrine. If America falls. An inflated and erroneous conception. Executive poppycock. This is the greatest country. Twist slowly. Right now the credibility. I was hoping. Two of the finest. We were all. An outrage. One senses a laxness. I am innocent. People have got to know. Scurrilous and inaccurate. "Brownshirt!" He must leave. I have passed the point. A throwback. The public is fed. It falls on us. Erasures occured. Coincidence, coincidence, coincidence. The truth is. I cannot vouch. Not a crook. Uncertainties make business. Not because they feel. Mounting his electronic throne. No one has been charged. Nobody is a friend. Make no mistake. I am not going to sit here.

You don't get to the top. In terms of morality. We assume politicians. A sour smell. He's the smartest guy. Just might have triggered. To call upon America. I'm against it! What we need now. This country, this country. I was not consulted. I think a president. At some point the United States. Not that person. A great nation. War continues. On the news. A daring show. You have to enforce. I recognize. Piano-key teeth, rep tie. When power. No single tradition. I'm certainly not appeased. Public enemy No.1. Americans no longer. Make a list. This country. A mess. One must believe. I saw a hand coming up.

Interlude of Being: Nothing on Either End of It

I can't ride a winged horse. Is nothing something?
A mermaid's fishy smell, point of a unicorn's horn.
I don't taste the sun.
Panic's nausea comes to naught. Sick tick
of the heart in a race with no one.
A plank-faced spook flying in my face.
Pluck out the eye if the eye offends you, leaving
an enucleated face, nothing to foresee.
About the dyadic world within, an undigested concept.
The less said the better. Nullity. Lacuna.
Gap, hole, cavity.

But I keep trying on nothing and it fits.
A bowl of nothing,
not even the desire to beg.
I'm in over my head. Harder still,
that tree needing a perceiver in the forest.
Cut and run. The question of the tree
always involves *does it grow to heaven*?
Or the body, sentient as a bag of sand.
I am in it nothing. Less beautiful
than a vase of lavender and wheat.
Vacuity. Nihilating. Nugatory.
O nothing, you nothing, *lui, lei, loro, niente*.
Do I toy with nothing or does nothing
toy with me. Carrying the barn on my back.
Rigor mortis is unimaginable
when a mosquito sucks at my ankle. If I forget
you, forget you, I think of you.
The spirit of the French woman's father returned
and all he said was *Open another bottle of wine*.
She was already drunk. All this velocity,

I'm used to it, how the day rotates on the speed
of its departure. The men in the square deal
a deck of strange cards. I'm turning over
all the paintings to find some original intention.
Days flat as a baking sheet.
I might as well be in Tiger, Georgia,
playing the ocarina on the porch.

Devotion

Good sun redeem my body quick
For I am sore from beating rain.
Redden me deep that I may dry
All the days you've been gone.
By grace, glad eye, I rise out of mire.
Cheat my soul of that black destroyer.
The rain said Nothing. Blister my back.
Death said Come so deftly. Good sun,
I'm skin, I'm live, I'm spared.
There's balm in my body yet.
Rush through, light guest, break up my blood.
By grace, by grace, I'll wash up whole.

III

> . . . it shone clearly distinct in the evening light, an impressive sight
> to the pilgrim. I contemplated it with the feelings due to an
> object that still has the power to make one travel so far.

Valley of the Assassins
Freya Stark

By the Mediterranean, Early Morning

Calm hour on a rock, breathing, like Tiresias,
Like Victoria who stayed here once, like any

Fisherman or child or ten-fingered, ten-toed
Soul the sea restores. Drawing back

The waves make a luscious sound, *Tyrrhenian*,
Tyrrhenian, sluicing through bright pebbles.

Astonishing, the tide, that I can *hear*,
All the plain wonders: Centuries of lives

Came before us, this rock fit them well;
Wonders, like the big hoop of time that landed me

On this travertine throne, glossy with salt water.
Clear to *see* and how elusive, the swelling curl—

To be *alive* inside fresh motion,
I rise, dive as it tips, runs,

Transparent, azure, over, riding
The leisurely curlicue of foam to shore.

Not a gullet with the mouth at one end opening
So the anus opens so the mouth opens,

But to marvel at the foil-bright
Brim of water falling over in light

That has just slid across Italy.
Now I let this wash my feet.

I have this thing called *life*.
It passes through something called *my body*.

Invitation

If you come you'll sit at the thick marble
table where I learned to mound flour
into a fountain and work in the egg.
You will wake to four calls of the cuckoo,
take coffee with the swaying
scent of wind roses and lilies. Like a wild
opium poppy, you'll open to the sun.
In the hot noons of baked stone
churches, I'll dip my finger
in holy water and cool your eyelids.
At twilight a dark gray deer,
with mossy horns and topaz eyes
will bite chicory at the edge of the field.
I'll show you a town washed at five with gold,
slick light gilding the stone street
and fine burnished faces like those
in illuminated texts under glass.

If you come, we'll walk down
the path in the vineyard where
I practice arias. In the travertine hot stream,
you'll see our feet gleam like Etruscan statues
unearthed after two thousand years. If you come
you will lie down in the bedroom
with five iron beds meant for curly haired girls
in long nightgowns with their dolls and board games.
When you won't sleep, we'll translate
the opening of *One Hundred Years of Solitude*
into Italian so all those you've forgotten
will come to your dreams,
calling secret names they knew you by.

When we come home late,
after rooms of Renaissance virgins
and dusty back roads from Umbertide
and Montepulciano, let's cook a pan of *ceche*,
small eels fried with garlic and sage.
Late in the kitchen we'll listen to
"A Whiter Shade of Pale" and
I'll show you how we used to dance at Southland.

When you come, trim the horse's mane,
pick sacks of plums, drive with me
to hill towns of round turrets and spilling
geraniums. You'll see the olives
the first day they are olives.
Like old peasants, we'll sit in the fireplace,
grilling slabs of bread and oil, pouring a young Chianti.
Feel the breeze rushing
around those hot grapes? If you come,
you'll come to coolness. In a shady
piazza, or under the fig tree where
two cats sleep, I'll start to tell you
something that once happened. Then I'll ask,
have I already told you this?
Yes, you'll say, yes, but it's different—
you've never told the story here before.

This Is the Music You Heard Once by a Lake

This is the music you heard once by a lake
where the sax seemed like water
in another form of motion. This is the music
called "our song" and when you asked,
the musician sang it in Italian, then German, then English;
this music made a small girl in blue shorts twirl.
You did not want to leave Italy or the fireflies' blinking
in synch with the synthesizer, pulsing this music
over the lake. You remember even what you don't
remember, terrazzo dance floor, the little lights' fandango,
this music, *you're doing well*, something your parents
could have heard the night your history began its beguine.
When your father asked *Who's that girl?* this music
fanned gypsy fires in their eyes.
Your parents are supple and bending into
this music you so clearly heard before you were born.
No, this is the schmaltz coming out of the loudspeaker
at the pizzeria where the ancient one, ignoring this music,
reads the news aloud to himself. This is summer,
windows open to the jasmine breeze, sending
this music uphill to the neighbor calling his dog,
you dancing alone on cool tiles, the sax
crawling up your backbone, this music
calling back someone you used to love, the one
always with you *in every summer place* where
this music stirred every drink with a pink flamingo swizzle.
You could sleepwalk through this tape of Fausto Papetti,
begin to dream of your daughter hearing this music
while shopping K Mart for grass seed and socks or
rising in the elevator at the Ritz in twenty years, thinking
this is the music my mother taught me to dance to
and another night comes back to her, when
she danced with the Latin man to this music,
a small town nightclub in California and he said
Hold your shoulders still and let your hips go.
This is the music they're always playing
because it plays you so well. It's *as if*,
as if *you are warm, you are real* in the music,
real-ly mine in the rain, even here, over the Tyrrhenian,

where you've never been before,
this music sifting over red geraniums, the sea below
then rolls, the patio where you never
sat in a thin green dress under this music,
testacoda in love—or maybe it was only a streaked
Florida sunset when you waited, only
this music to know, not the transmigrated soul or
the doggy dog life but *so rare* the riffs
that take you back to all the music
that takes you back. *At last*
the sax flows through you via Fausto Papetti,
this music selling you not to the devil but down the river
of full moony nights when *he* always will walk over, always
in his yellow shirt, saying his name, pulling you into this music.

The Long Bony Cats of Montecatini

don't expect petting. They sleep
by day under cars or saunter
the ramparts. Some are missing ears,
others half their tails, and they are
oddly marked—one all white except
a triangle of stripes on her head,
like a graft from a wilder type.
Alley brawlers, all.
At two A.M. their horrifying cries
begin, like children having their nails
pulled out with pliers. I'm afraid
I've screamed in my sleep again,
that stopped sound I can't make
that finally breaks from my throat
when the man is coming down the hall
bare, sweaty and grinning or
old with one eye and a shovel. They whiz
down the hill yowling, a pack of cats,
tumble spitting down the tile roofs
so intent on fight they fall—
there's silence then, they're stunned
apart, or dead. Who are their owners?
Where are their saucers? They're wild
miniature tigers and leopards stalking.
That jungle-marked skinny thing next door
walks like a dog and carries a live
bird in her jaw. She crouches unmoving
as I walk by, wishing it were I
she had her teeth in. Every night
peace breaks apart in the valley,
night opens, and Death, who
has hid in the shut medieval granary
opens the door. Someone is having
an operation without anesthesia,
torture begins in Central American jails,
napalm burns off an arm and leg, but
then I see the moonlight
on the pots of geraniums, soft fog
where the hills cup.

It's only the cats. They run their music
backwards. They're in deep dispute
over socialism, birth control,
corruption in high places, love, the lack
of night life for cats in Montecatini.

Ninnananna from Rignano

While you flew, an owl lit on the window sill.
Could he hear the whir of mice over brown furrows?
I was afraid—your plane might turn wing up, begin
to spin down, split, free fall through black night,
into the blacker ocean, sending your pure
face to float on top of eternity. Oh, yes,

I'm prey to that terror a birth guarantees—
the world is a barbed snare, one small red
berry a poison on the tongue. Even
a stone house can shake down as you strain
to outrun the speed of stairs falling
behind you, oh, yes, the root of courage is *heart*.
When you were new, close enough
to hear your hair growing, I told you

the world is a miracle made out of nothing,
absolutely nothing. I looked in
as you slept, listened for your breathing.
Your small hip curved smooth as a bowl,
your eyes roved through easy dreams.
The hooves of all the horses
that threw you missed your skull, kindly
scraped your shoulder or bruised

your thigh, and your friend horribly
caught the force as the two of you
shoved your bikes in front of a speeding
car; when the half ton chunk of overhead
freeway fell as you sped down the FDR,
crushing not yours but someone's bones and light,

you were merely caught in traffic, impatient
to be home. My nymph, slipknot
in the heart, the inverse square law
that your father told you holds
the universe intact, held you
safe from stress cracks, bombs
and hijacks. All afternoon
you sleep like the child you were
in the turned iron bed with a medallion

of Mary and beasts at peace. I fear
a thousand threats and this afternoon can
clip an armful of Queen Anne's lace
because you arced the waters, appeared,
abruptly at Gate 4, fresh and tired.
We have stone walls four-hundred-years thick.
All day it will stay 8:14 on the clock
with its carved horse rearing.
Nothing will fall except
the plums with soft thuds in the grass.
You sleep so long. What luck—
the bed's sweet squeak. Cream thickens
in the pitcher for blackberries when you wake,
with your famous smile, sultry cheeks,
your dangerous feet cool on the brick stairs.

Waiting for Grace (Believing in Waters)

1.

Not a jewelled madonna found afterwards
in the heart. Not grandiosity, dread, pills,
weepiness, guilt, old Bordeaux, stalling,
lust, flailing. No sucking the wound
while ascending the sky,
no eating of supplicants' pus and lice.

And yes, *the night was long and deep, valentine.*

(madonna
valentine

2.

Asking for something pure under the trees as
the white bowl of limes casts a slate
of shadow on my hand. Asking for
a certain elasticity *in the gray area
between body and mind, clarity and blood.*

(lime, slate
clarity, blood

Again to seek to gain to win something—outcropping
of desire, like a death causes admiring
return to the self. Desire, the easy roll
of a green beetle in the rose,
her pillowy pink, her fragrance as strong
as a snap of my fingers: I'm here, I'm here.

(desire, green
rose

3.

What if there's nothing to put
in the empty place, the dry amphora chased with nymphs
and gods. *There's just the everyday
wildness of the woods.* And under emptiness—
something atrocious remaining (unlike clear tragedy,
the boy's dive in the stream severing his spine)
a pulling through the long tunnel downhill, leading
to the lake where everyone remembers
a great strategical victory or a defeat in fog.

(nymphs, gods

(victory
wildness

I dig up terra cotta fragments of pots, plates
in the garden, and a running horse not stopped
by rust. I touch the continuum:
they made something,
served forth polenta and boar.

(horse
continuum

So name the sloop Primavera, she will slide
over the water and another language casts a charm.   (sloop, charm

4.
The Holy Milk in the reliquary equals three ghetto kids
in New York hell, swaying on the corner
singing "We Are the World." All the innocent light   (holy, reliquary
on the rose where the beetle waves his legs,   talent,
on Sarah's fourth day of rigor mortis on the floor,   morning
hungry cat weaving his tail around her foot.
Her talent, her problem, her putrefaction, and
morning so fully morning, birds, dew, and all.

5.
In the unlit passageway between the madonnas
in Città di Castello, *flagrante delicto*,
Zeus rides Leda. His beak biting her right nipple,
his swany body hooked at her pelvis, she takes
the thrust. At this moment, it is not about the empire.
His blood pumping to the very edge of her body.
In the humid corridor, her face has peeled away.
Outside, children sell crafts   (children
for the relief of other children in Peru.

6.
I could try to abide on the wafer alone.
Thin to transparency. Once I had a vision
so I understand the saint who found
the foreskin of Jesus materialized in her mouth.
It was just daylight far in the country.
I was totally emptied.   (vision, notes
I heard a high singing in the sky,   ravished
almost a screech but beautiful, the notes going
higher, higher than a human voice, almost
unbearable. I lay in bed listening,
saying you're not the type for this,
this, this record amplified from somewhere?
But where? I wanted it to end
but time slowed, as during an earthquake.
The singing, as the saints say,
ravished me. When it stopped I stood up.
A red towel hung over the balcony,   (towel, sun
soaking in the sun.

7.
The body is breachable. And don't the gods
throw mist in our eyes to keep us from knowing
what's divine? When the penis absolutely
radiates, big as Texas, where's doubt? Let's go.   (divine, penis
Another day, I'll pursue the incognito.   incognito

8.
Bless the rain. The two hyperventilating rabbits
at the Saturday market get another week
before being stuffed with *pancetta* and herbs,
roasted with potatoes and rosemary. Delicious,   (delicious
the fat and the good bread.   fur
One splotched, one brown. (In the butcher's case,
stripped and stretched, a rabbit's eyes bulge.
Fur on the tail proves it not cat.)
They nestle (don't name them) in the box of straw,
my hand stroking their damp fur backs.

9.
Measure the urine into a beaker and wait
for the mineral content analysis. A quantity
of water from the thermal source will balance,
replace, reorganize humors. The body's   (wait, water, humors
minerals, a microcosm of earth's. True,
I store in liver and spleen the same proportion
as Africa's and New Zealand's mines
bear zinc and potassium. Save the flawless
stones excreted with hot pain.
The cure is a month (believing in waters)
of taking measured sips, bed rest, long walks, cards   (cure, Vergil, bees
in the evening with others who need the cure.   perfume
Under the small ring of light at the bedside,
read Vergil, who thought bees generated
spontaneously, the same bees that outside
the window burrow in the lime trees' dime store perfume.

10.
I want to put my finger on it.
Was it grace when Zeus besotted her?
Grace, a veil floating toward earth. Grace
falling down over fate. We tend to see with stern   (grace, grace
impersonality, not the feathery torque of his neck,   (fate, neck, god

46

the squawk, flap, stringy bird erection, the beak
clamping over her nipple. This is the visit of a god?

11.
Back home, that solace of place, that ace of hearts.
Not the mace canister, not the panic button
good one-hundred yards from front door. Neither
the brace on the back door nor the trouble
signal nor warning stickers on windows.
Not the Pakistani grocer on the corner   (solace, place, ace
beaten with a crowbar and not his wife
screaming and not my shaking finger punching 911.
Not the naked woman opening her legs
in a window on Divisidero, not the glazed man
on Fillmore shouting he wants to stick it
in some pussy. Neither the whisper
to give me your wallet nor my cracked jaw afterward.

And not the exhibitionist in the rhododendron dell,
stepping from behind each height of bloom,
especially the speckled pink flowers
that reminded me of a dotted Swiss pinafore
I wore the summer I was nine, his green pants open,
his horse-sized exhibit A purple and engorged.
Not his smile. Not me saying Oh, my God.   (bloom, God

Not the ski-masked face staring in the window.

12.
Blood sticks to the work, Goethe said.
Our blood, rabbit blood, the magic blood
of wine transformed? The blood handprint
on the cave wall for 40,000 years? The "blood
jet" of poetry? The blood that is the first sign?
The blood the health teacher said is the womb's
tears at the failure to conceive? Bloody mess
of chicken guts steaming in the garbage,
streak on my thigh I thought was plum juice?
Bloody Mary, the girl I love?
When the blood money is paid. When the bloodmobile
has pulled off. When the blood pudding congeals.
When the bloodworm reaches
the bloodroot. When I'm in the blood bath.

When I'm pale from the bloodletting.
When the blood is shot, sucked, stained, shed.
Waiting for grace, I'm cold-blooded, inching
from surface to surface. Blood: loosely,
the dictionary says, life.   (life

13.
Lift, wind scented with lime,

lift my hair off my forehead,

and if I am pleistocene,

lift my hair from my baked face,

for the four o'clock sun's

sifting gold and it falls

over the rift of hills,

over my shoulders, hard

as the swaying pears,

if I am medieval, lift

my eyes, the sheer air

veils those holy beings

the cypress trees, skims

the dip of hills, I'm here

on the terrace, heiress

and laundress of swells

of light in the pear tree

lift and let spin the leaves,

down the fruit will fall,

warm plum wind, lime wind,

gold wind starts turning

all the pinwheels

in the body, blond light

also a fluid

circulated by the heart.

14.
Bony girl
in glasses

on a white bicycle rolling
through the park,
silver sparking
around her ankles,

*(bony
world
over*

her lips
say something
over and over
to herself,

passes within two feet,
I step out of her way,
doesn't see me.

the lines in italics are from poems by Ashley King

Ancient Air: A Stony Sestina, Doubled in Time

Someone left a rose on Dante's stone.
The woman who keeps his grounds speaks, as if remembering
a quirky neighbor who died last year.
Old quiet heart of an empire, Ravenna.
Twenty years ago I saw slides of the blue and gold
mosaics, heard the professor say, "San Vitale, Galla Placidia,

Theodora, Justinian." Flashes in the dark, Galla Placidia's
heaven-blue dome, the wild touch of the east on Italian stone.
I thought *I must go to Ravenna.* Christ in a field of gold
and water, like some trick the artist worked with memory:
See, water is transparent though it's hard aqua tile. Ravenna,
ancient maze, flat coast sopped with more pollution every year.

Dante loved this pine forest. Walked his exile years
and never lost his way. Imagine him staring at Galla Placidia's
starry tomb. I would not like to die in Ravenna,
a dirty little city with miracles. Sun falling hard on stone.
I wake up late, thinking of "Degrees of Gray in Phillipsburg." Remember
Hugo reading *isn't this your life?* What gold

in that rough ore? He assumed we'd answer yes. But now this gold.
We quicken too fast with loss. True images imprint for years,
forever, will loosen me from my small fates, from bare memory.
Isn't *this* my life? The blue intricate dome of Galla Placidia
rivals any night sky in my history. Dante lies with his stony
sestina, hells, *paradiso*, his *vita nuova* in this Ravenna

as still as he would anywhere. And this remains Ravenna,
robust with glory. Twenty-two virgins in white, a scaled gold
progression through my mind over twenty years. In the stone
asymmetry of San Vitale, the organ begins, expanding space. Years
ago I heard this music, it falls like the hand of God. The placid
father would sacrifice the child. Don't I hear this in memory,

music, stopping loss. Arresting the moment. Memory
jolts at this skewed octagon, apse off to the side. In Ravenna
the mosaic hand of God comes down through music. This place,
grayer than shades of Phillipsburg. I answer Hugo *no.* The gold
tesserae dazzles when I bring *luce* with my *lire.* From their years
they send something new to the world. A twisting welter of stone

streets, my feet catch fire. Sandal rubbing blisters, stone-
bruised heels. The tourist map says keep walking, some memory
of the original Roman plan persists. Procession of years
to get me here, some red thread in the labyrinth. Ravenna
in rain. Isn't this my life? All the fierce black eyes, gold
backgrounds. That music *would* begin in this place.

Continuous motions the mind can make. Poets dead in swampy places
and American mountains. I wake up turning Hugo's poem, like a stone
with my foot, in Hotel Byron's anonymous room. But on the blue-gold
globe in the dome sits Christ flanked by angels. I remember
Yeats, how smart to say *intellect*: the great mosaics of Ravenna
shine not to unaging belief, but to the gusto of the mind, year

after year, for the present. Those Byzantines stare over years,
still come forth from their time, having the force to placate
fate by standing among legends. I have blisters in Ravenna.
Oh, replace my shoes with the sandals of virgins on stone,
walking the eternal grass of the window wall above my memory
of the wise men just as they are. The Byzantines ring the gold

dome undefeated. Otherwise, what's the use of art, of gold.
I still walk to Dante's tomb, remember he was nine years
old when he saw Beatrice, eight, in crimson, a bead of memory
he carried to exile. That, and himself. He was not displaced.
I came because the black-rimmed eyes with remote, stony
stares startled me in Art 206. And I always thought of Ravenna

at a distance. Justinian offers the bread of life to Ravenna,
And lovely Theodora pours scarlet wine—the gold
laid irregularly to catch light—from the high stones.
I'll never be back. The light in my hotel room was spent years
ago. I came like a lost cousin to visit Galla Placidia,
ready at last to know they all continue forth from the past. Memory,

the mad bicycles on these tangled streets, memory,
constellation in mosaic with water rushing over, blue as Ravenna
when summer rain dries on glassy tile and sun returns a placid
day. Clack of this dialect in Dante's ear and mine. Vigorous golden
sun. I wrote in my notebook *Ravenna finally this year.*
Bought shoes. So glad. Maybe I've left all stones

unturned. *Isn't this your life?* Inklings of memory laid like gold
in the mosaic dome of the skull, finding deep Ravenna, for years
unknown, bold eyes of Theodora glittering in this place of stone.

Come Slowly, Eden

I wish Federico would come around with the honey.
Four cool apricots on the stone sill. I go on
slowly translating: *Truths that go.*
A young breeze blows on my face.
Below in the field, a man holds
a rabbit's hind legs taut
and his boy peels back fur
like a woman rolling down
a thick stocking. The rabbit is lean
and pitifully stretched into full-out
running position. Is that correct,

truths that go?
The solid sound of thunder. Heat lightning.
Big splats of rain strike the terrace, clay
soaking in rain, taking a shine.
And far off on the hills, the rival sun
hits wheat fields in struts of light.
The house is medieval, medieval,
I say over and over, a charm
against getting struck.

The terrace dries, is set for the great meal,
Avremo (we will have), *ho avuto* (I had).
I'm living with the basic verbs.
Grilled veal, white beans off the pole one hour
in crushed garlic, oil, and sage,
real bread called *ciabatta* (slipper), and tomatoes
almost too red.

I want memory crushed
down hard into layers, I want it to transform
into unscratchable brightness.
I don't have centuries to wait.
Here I concentrate hard on paradise, make
un bel falo di tutto che riguardi
(a beautiful bonfire of all that I regarded).
A scorpion runs black and sideways down the kitchen drain.
The foreign words yield, as when I
held up a candle to scan for secrets
written in disappearing ink.

Now, the bells' random clattering.
Sometimes I don't hear the hour, then
suddenly it clangs close, an old woman
beating a dishpan next to my ear.
At twilight, the hundred acrobat swallows
do their daredevil swoops, nosedives,
short glides after gnats, then
they're gone. I like to materialize
in the piazza, a person who arrived whole last week
with no prior existence or disaster.
The gold sun wheels over the wheat.
The sky a washed fresco too far faded to restore.
Swallows arrow into holes
in the ramparts some medieval mason
shaped for them with his thumb.
Flesh is grass—a metaphor so easy
it must not be true.

Rome, August 5

Sultry sleep, no good, covering up what, the real dreams. Rip of an ambulance blast, startled day returns like a headline, the assassin barely out of childhood. Yes, last day here, hard rush of thought weighed down by heat. Waking feels like sinking. What was the one word scrawled on a white wall? The elation of light in our shuttered room, the light in a novel, seeping into walls lined with ancient columns, lions, perspectives, the Genovese proverb, *light is half a companion.* A fly squished in the matting.

Whinnying elevator on raveling cords. Afternoon below, with water pouring through a dolphin's mouth, and stones taking the heat. You, with me now, slender as the letter l, as a carnation stem floating in the fountain. So other, your mouth with irregular stars and chandeliers. Movies under your eyelids, arias of the past. A feeling inside of. We are briefly August in Roma, with waiters and blue dust in churches.

A tilted mirror, my face hidden from me. Shocking, only yours to see in busy sleep. My peeling skin, a layer of summer off. Your love. Confirming like a rain on Sunday. You are the color of honey from bees who fed on sunflowers and wind. Pliant. A precious wing. Imagine the truth, the span of my hand on your hot shoulder. Slowly the sun thickens in the room. The bed low, with sky, oh, that's best, light cut in ingots. Summer is closing, the handmade broom on the farm terrace already slants behind us in the landscape. Those weeks, we took the imprint: dry summer mornings, barefoot on tiles powdery with fine dust. Every day, deeper, every day, the forward pitch of summer, wasps whirring in the pears, as in the classical texts. Corridor of shade down through chestnuts I love, though now only in the mind.

We are like ourselves, or maybe more. Slowly more, as Leonardo used old stained walls. See, now we always will be there, reflected by countless surfaces—the well goes low, fields at evening melt into a dusty gold wash, our horses shift down through steep rocks with stiffened forelegs. Your horse wants mine, another occasion for laughter. So much laughter surprises me. I don't know if I'll come to Italy again. We were soaked in the heat rains. My old life tries to right itself. Recurrent fear of a swamped boat comes back and back at night: I am just below my need for air.

You smile when I say these thoughts. I'm taken on faith. I lean back, so comfortable on the afternoon, darned linen sheet, ordinary, my feet, *there,* opposite, friendly. The farm stretches over three soft hills and into friezes— whistle of scythe in wheat, the worker's whoop to warn vipers. Geese pulling their white skirts along with them. Now the sun has travelled. The shape of thinking will arc up over countries, oceans and down into the familiar.

I said you *can* touch the world. Lilac spray over the door. Cold nose of the baby fox in the ditch. There, day bending. Because I had to start over, my life having emptied. I had to fill it up. My hands mounding fava beans on the kitchen table, you on a yellow towel, showing your body to the sun, all the papers from my desk blowing around the room.

When Rain Pulls the Wind off the Arno at Night

Thunder booms through the house like waves boom
at sea when the mast is a twig, booms
like the avalanche that took Vera at Annapurna,
riveting her blue jacket to a crevice of ice,
like my father's voice
                              warning me not
to bathe when it thunders,
lightning waits to strike girls
with pearly toes and sunburned shoulders, and
will split the room, lift the tub
and my white hide to the sky;
                              a flash divides
the night in my closed eyes, the sky
a bare dendritic slide of winter birch—
what long roots dangle. I hold my breath.
But isn't it good, the gigantic storm?
Waking to the flood of terror they felt
by fire in the caves? I find a match
but the candle displaces the dark
only half way up the wall. I ricochet home—
sheet lightning in the South.
                              I used to
lie on the ground, letting rain
soak through me, feeling each bright
burst of forked silver.
Quick wind parts the bedroom shutters,
and strands and loops of rain
pool on desk and floor.

Rain flaying the grapes, rain filling the mouths
of the dead so they stop their endless chatter.
Was I dreaming of my mother rinsing
my tangle of hair with a bowl of rainwater?
How do I lie here seven thousand years
from home? How are the mares? Where are
the six dumb guinea hens?
                              All ride
the earth lightly, a brief inflorescence.
What did that refrain mean, "cleft for me," rising
perpendicular from the white board church in Georgia?

Bolts spear the ground, crack along my backbone.
The road in is a river. All fuses blown.
Shutters could twirl over the fields,
bolts peel off my body, leave me foreign,
clean-stripped, borne, electric.

Lighting Candles to the Household Gods

1

Hot willow sticks woven into a brown basket, round for cherries until the juice stains and it's emptied and placed in the sun.

2

The retarded boy imitates the flag throwers from Arezzo. He soars when flags are tossed, body revolving with the colors and furlings. We politely applaud the corps. He surges and exults. Soon I am watching him and not the performance. He does not smile, it's more than that. He leans into the action, his being exactly where he is. He is thick, with hooded eyes like an iguana; his soul is an airy helix, constantly escaping through the rib cage.

3

When the dog's heart was opened, we saw long worms like spaghetti. The sturdy muscle clutched and unclutched while the packed worms squirmed as worms will and wove themselves around each other. There was a small hope, the doctor said, pulling out wet shoelaces, throwing them in a stainless steel bowl. A blue solution might destroy the worms of the heart. Then pills forever. The dog might leap in our arms again or wallow in dung, might come in covered with sandspurs, and wet the rug for joy when we arrive home. We were sick at seeing inside her ventricles. When the dog woke up with a clean heart, her eyes roamed, she didn't risk a wag or scratch and we feared even then, secretly, another worm might be turning.

4

You cannot fall down the new well. It's only as round as your face and drops 300 feet to a pump—close to the inferno but the water is cold. It must be tested for minerals and amoeba that could infest the colon. And we thought because it was new and cost a lot it was surely pure. In other days you could run through a field and fall into a well and never get out, no one could hear you trying to scale the slimy stone walls, no one could hear your cries or see the snake spiraling in the water. Wells were made for water and to fall into. The new well is not even a well, it's a *pozzo* because something created solely in another language does not translate as *well*. We're adaptable. We will have a stone wall around it so it looks like a well.

5

Don't buy the raffle ticket; you don't *want* to win the two live geese at the fair. (Good luck of roaming geese, their downy underfeathers for your face pillow.) You came within *one number* of winning the donkey, for Christ's sake. Let's just eat and leave.

6

The agribusiness fields of giant sunflowers bloom at once, each flower as big as a human face fringed with outrageous gold. We have to pull over every few miles and stare as far as the eye curving over the hills. How can this be? This is a crop: the astounding beauty of these flowers doing about face to the sun. On hot days they droop a little, hanging their heads as though exhausted at field duty. They're making oil for fried zucchini flowers and potatoes. Each, the paradigm sunflower, though the Italian name is right, *girasole*, the turning built in. There are *not* too many of us who follow the sun, they reply to Yeats. When we evolve, this is the standing army of our dreams.

7

One would be enough; we found too many whelks and conchs on that pre-lapsarian beach, spiral shells with dawn colored nacreous inward curves. We picked up one after another—look at this, completely white and perfect, the points of the large spiral intact, sharp as cat's incisors. Six miles, empty except for shells strewn from tideline to the dunes. We never were so stunned by a place. Lavender ones with streaks of pink like melted crayons, hundreds of new shells, one inch, three inches long, and several giants, big enough to prop open a door. How could we carry them and what would we do with them at home? We picked up hundreds of angel wings, scallops, sand dollars. We decided on specimens. As we walked, we discarded our formerly perfect ones time after time until, when we returned to the path to the house, we had nothing. We decided on nothing. Nothing, out of endless choices. Walking home we saw an alligator rise from the brack, open his jaws, as in a cartoon. We ran through the mosquitoes, laughing, over the marsh path. A small whelk bounced out of the cuff of my shorts.

8

The turning radius of an ox determined the width of the terraces on the hill-side but now there is no white ox in the stall though his manger still is there, the wood rubbed down where he leaned over to eat, and forty years or more later, his uric acid still causes a fluffy white mold when it rains, and we get a whiff of him and almost can touch his sweaty haunch and hear him shudder. The way we wind up the hill to the view of the lake and valley, we follow his formal turnings, an old cursive gently following the fold of the hills and the way returns and rolls to go forward but the motion is up, suddenly we're surprised to be on the higher level.

9

Trees are waltzing at 5:20 A.M. The courtly old-world lindens already feel the *summum bonum* of the bees, a string quartet that will last all day while they ride the waxy flowers in the breeze. For oaks on the terraces, there's only the two-step, back and back, and the cypresses in mourning keenly sway, the green-dark cones seeping blue to the air. The volunteer plums are good at the twist, a ghost of Chubby Checker tosses them while they stand in place. Only the olives don't dance. Their rippling shiver of supple green stirs just enough to turn up silver underleaves. The olives at dawn look as though they might revert to ancient crones, or so I think at 5:20 when the flexuous lindens flounce three-quarter time into morning.

Lines for Massimo

A black column of women walks into the cypress lane. Closer, I see their cellophane-covered flowers, then, between trees, glimpse the hearse. Caught in a string of cars winding downhill with dusty light on the sunflower fields, I'm going to the shoe supermarket to buy hiking boots (and it closes soon); I'm listening to break-your-heart arias by Puccini on a tape that baked and curled in the glove compartment. The tremolo vibrates in my blood. Yes, I saw the black-edged death notices stuck on the wall in Cortona, the death notice for Massimo, 16, beloved son and brother of, beloved student of, beloved grandson of, then the mention in the bar that the boy didn't take the turn on his Vespa. An Irish mother on the news runs through me screaming with grief for her gunned-down boy, her body so stiff four people bore it aloft like a plank.

Such a plain afternoon, winding toward Castiglion Fiorentino. In the Lake of Nemi, the mirror of Diana, a diver in 1446 saw two ancient ships lying on the muddy bottom. Another diver in 1535 went down in a bell, and another in 1827 used a raft with hoists, then someone in 1895 succeeded in bringing up bronze animals, a Medusa head and a large flat hand, along with pieces of mosaic decking. The cars turn in to the *cemetario* and I speed up with a search for Massimo, summer waiter at the trattoria. Did he forget the bread and misadd the bill that night? He won't live out his life in this noble town. What God, as a kindness, killed Hera's son so he would never fade? That flawed idea travelled too far. Their backs are bent. This is their sad day, and a pregrief ripples through my shoulders for bad days sure to come. Last hour for Massimo. Before he begins a long residence under the ground.

Finally, Mussolini hauled the boats out by pumping the volcanic lake down by 72 feet. The strange, ancient ships proved to be enormous: 66 x 234 feet and 78 x 239 feet. They surpassed anyone's fantasy: decks of polychrome marble and mosaic, fluted marble columns, heated baths, copper nails hammered in during the reign of Caligula. Technical ingenuity such as pump pistons, pulleys, and platforms on ball bearings no one, even now, knows the use of. A canted anchor still had its knot, neatly tied by a Roman sailor. Floating temples? Pleasure palaces? No one knows the purpose of these magical vessels, miraculously brought up from the waters.

Massimo's hearse of roses and yellow gladioli, profligate with blossoms; it soothes the eye, the woven flower coverlet we call a blanket. Do we bring flowers to the dead because they too are lovely and soon to die? Or more practically, in old times, to mask the rot of corpse? These switchback curves. Smear of his face on asphalt. In 1944 the retreating Germans entered the museum and wantonly burned the ships. After all that time, they simply were gone.

Such a plain afternoon. Cat sleeping on top of the garbage can while a rat scours the ground. I buy brown suede boots with laces, then I pick up groceries and see in the freezer glass how ordinary I look. Buying supplies for Sunday. Potato gnocchi, white peaches, just ripe. Warm weight of peach in my hand. Every gesture over and gone. A leaching heat. I push the cart to the car. Up the hill again, close to the Porta Romana, two women, heads bent into the climb, walk away from the funeral. One drops to her knees and the other leans down and spreads her black scarf. They are gathering for their supper the young arugula growing wild on the roadside. I pass a flash of gap-toothed smile.

Shaving my Legs with Ockham's Razor

From the dream world of paradigms
        I took the water slide: a decade of realism

Brings me to William, his steady truth
        that the world proceeds case by case.

Take my legs—winter pale, glowing like white
        neon. The long bone an arctic ledge

Propped and glistening on the tub—
        William could have regarded them, instead of Plato's beard

That never could come off. Every three days, I lather
        the faint stubble, dip my disposable razor:

If less is enough, why do more?
        He must have honed his razor on a thick strop.

I'm steeped these late sensible years
        in his principle of parsimony, so close to parsnip and parson.

There once was a paradigm! My legs tanned and oiled.
        Shaved daily—such perfection:

Buttered in summer with coconut oil,
        (toenails scarlet), slicked in winter with lotions.

Moreover, what to say about that ultra-idealist, Aunt Emmy,
        who plucked out each hair on her legs with tweezers:

Never shave; it will grow back thick and black.
        I watched to see if her pores enlarged but no,

When the creamy pegnoir fell to the side I saw her calves
        silky firm and slim. *Suffer for beauty*, she said.

But William, after my father's, I borrowed your razor!
        A straightedge. Your cool, fetid breath in my face:

Plurality is not to be assumed without necessity.
        My legs in perfection at Bowen's Mill swimming pool.

My legs at the end of exhausting winter, daikon roots.
        William, old heretic, you died

The Black Death, that quick wasting. I would like to get out
        Of this tub. Scraped clean, I will slip into a skirt

With a flounce and walk down the white road into town.
        Oil of narcissus on my pulse points, radiating *more is more*.

Etruscan Head

You, plowing,
turn up a marble head
in the furrow. It is 1790
and raining. She broke true
at the neck, looks back
at the sky with eyes
emptied of time older than
the Romans. Nose sheared
but the bridge high and fine,
the mouth like the mouth
of the nervy village girl
who steals your grapes and cuts
her eyes at you.
Sweat runs down your back.
The head has come up
clean. It feels fresh and
heavy in your hands. What to do
with the broken beauty of the past?
You place the head
on an olive stump and under
the rain she begins to shine,
heroic, moon pure, your dead
daughter's forehead, a peel
of wax on the cathedral floor.
Your clothes stink and steam.
Now you take the plow and
follow the hillside. Two hundred
years later I will see her
in the Volterra museum.
My grandmother's blind eyes
come back to stare. I would
like to hold the head, I
think her shoulders
would feel like mine.
Somewhere under the vineyards
I imagine perfect hard
hands and sandaled feet.
We're not mistaken about our lives.

Frances Mayes grew up in Fitzgerald, Georgia. Her books of poetry are *Sunday in Another Country* (The Heyeck Press), *After Such Pleasures* (Seven Woods Press), *The Arts of Fire* (The Heyeck Press), and *Hours* (Lost Roads Publishers). Her poems have been published in *Atlantic Monthly*, *Antioch Review*, *Iowa Review*, *New American Writing*, *New England Review*, *North American Review*, *Poetry*, and many other literary magazines. She is also the author of *The Discovery of Poetry*, a popular college textbook recently published in a second edition by Harcourt Brace. Her autobiographical essays have appeared in *American Poetry Review*, *Frontiers: A Journal of Women's Studies*, *Gettysburg Review*, *Ironwood*, *The Virginia Quarterly Review*, *Southern Review*, *The New York Times*, *American Scholar*, *Ploughshares* and elsewhere. In 1996, Chronicle Books will publish *In the Country of the Sun*, a nonfiction book on Italy, where she lives part of the year. She is chair of the Creative Writing Department at San Francisco State University. She also directed The Poetry Center there for several years. A National Endowment for the Arts fellowship was awarded to her in 1988.

Book design and typesetting by Peter Armitage
Set in Birch and Berkeley Book
Printed and bound by McNaughton and Gunn